MATT PHILIE

How To Get Sponsored

Brand Deals, Free Products, and How Sponsorships Work

UPLOAD

First published by UPLOAD LLC 2026

Copyright © 2026 by Matt Philie

All rights reserved. No part of this publication may be reproduced, stored, or transmitted in any form or by any means, electronic, mechanical, photocopying, recording, scanning, or otherwise without written permission from the publisher. It is illegal to copy this book, post it to a website, or distribute it by any other means without permission.

Second edition

This book is for every creator who started with zero subscribers and a stubborn belief that this could become something real. I was once that kid too. If you give this your full effort, obsess over getting better, and stay in it longer than most people are willing to, the results will surprise you. Amazing things happen when you take your work seriously and refuse to quit.

Contents

Introduction		1
1	Understanding Brand Deals and How They Actually Work	7
2	When You Can Start Charging and How Creators Actually...	20
3	How to Price Yourself Without Guessing	29
4	Creating a Media Kit That Actually Works	40
5	Cold Outreach That Actually Gets Replies	51
6	Finding the Right Contact Without Wasting Time	62
7	Handling Inbound Emails and Qualifying Brand Interest	72
8	Agreements, Contracts, and Protecting Yourself	80
9	Getting Paid Without Chasing	90
10	Delivering Content Without Losing Control	98
11	Reporting Results and Getting Rebooked	107
12	Maintaining Relationships and Building a Sustainable...	115
13	Making Money Without Selling Out	124
14	The Long Game and Final Takeaways	132
About the Author		140

Introduction

Why This Book Exists (and Why You Can Trust It)

If you're reading this, there's a good chance you fall into one of three groups.

- You're a creator who wants brand deals but doesn't know where to start.
- You're already working with brands, but it feels inconsistent, awkward, or underpriced.
- Or you're doing deals now and want to stop guessing and start operating like a professional.

This book exists because none of those problems are caused by talent.

They're caused by a lack of clear information.

Who I Am and Why I Wrote This

My name is Matt Philie. I've been creating content on the internet since I was a kid, long before brand deals were normalized and long before creators were treated like businesses.

Over the years, I've:

- Built and grown multiple YouTube channels
- Worked with hundreds of brands across tech, lifestyle, software, and consumer products
- Negotiated everything from free product to long-term paid partnerships
- Seen how deals are handled on the creator side and the brand side

I've been the small creator brands took a chance on.

I've been the mid-sized creator agencies chased.

I've been the creator who said yes too early, charged too little, and learned the hard way.

I've also been the creator who learned how to:

- Price work confidently
- Say no without guilt
- Build repeat brand relationships
- Turn sponsorships into predictable income instead of random wins

This book is not theory. It's not recycled advice. It's what actually happens when emails are sent, contracts are signed, and money is on the line.

This Is Not a "Get Rich" Book

If you're looking for shortcuts, this is the wrong book.

Brand deals are not magic. They are business relationships.

This book will not promise:

- Overnight success
- Guaranteed income
- Viral growth
- Easy money

What it will give you is clarity.

Clarity around:

- How brands actually think
- How deals are structured
- How creators lose leverage
- How to protect yourself
- How to build something sustainable

If you apply what's here, results come faster. If you ignore it, mistakes get more expensive.

Who This Book Is For

This book is written for:

- New creators with small but real audiences
- Micro-creators who get ignored by brands
- Established creators who feel underpaid
- Anyone tired of guessing how sponsorships work

It does not matter what platform you're on.

It does not matter how many followers you have.

If you have an audience and want to work with brands without losing your voice, this applies to you.

What Makes This Book Different

Most sponsorship advice falls into two extremes.

One side oversimplifies everything.

The other side over complicates it with jargon and theory.

This book sits in the middle.

It explains:

- What to do
- Why it matters
- What happens if you don't
- How to respond when things go sideways

No fluff. No motivational filler. Just reality.

How to Use This Book

This is important.

You can read this book straight through.

But it's designed to be used, not just read.

Each chapter gives you:

- Core concepts
- Real-world context
- Practical guidance

At the end of most chapters, you'll find:

- Frameworks to help you make decisions
- Checklists to avoid common mistakes
- Playbook sections with examples you can reuse

You don't need to memorize everything. You need to know where to look when something comes up.

That's intentional.

One Final Thing Before We Start

You don't need permission to take yourself seriously.

Brands already treat sponsorships like business.

The moment you do the same, everything changes.

This book is here to help you cross that line confidently, without burning bridges or selling out.

Let's get into it.

1

Understanding Brand Deals and How They Actually Work

Before you worry about pitching, pricing, contracts, or media kits, you need to understand what a brand deal actually is. Most creators don't struggle with sponsorships because they are bad at content. They struggle because they misunderstand the relationship entirely.

A brand deal is not a reward.

It is not a favor.

It is not validation.

It is a business transaction where attention, trust, and creative execution are exchanged for money, product, or both.

Once you internalize that, everything else in this book becomes easier.

Why creators get sponsorships wrong

Most creators approach brand deals emotionally. Brands approach them operationally.

Creators think in terms of:

- "Am I big enough?"
- "Do they like my content?"
- "What if I ask for too much?"
- "I don't want to scare them away."

Brands think in terms of:

- What problem are we trying to solve?
- What channel fits this campaign?
- What risk are we taking?
- What alternatives exist if this doesn't work?

This disconnect is why creators either undercharge, overdeliver for free, or feel taken advantage of. It is also why some creators with relatively small audiences make consistent sponsorship income, while others with huge followings struggle.

Brands do not wake up hoping to sponsor someone. They wake up trying to hit metrics.

Your job is not to "get sponsored."

Your job is to be a useful solution.

How brands actually see creators

To a brand, you are not just a person with followers. You are one option in a list that might include:

- Paid social ads
- Influencer agencies
- Production studios
- User generated content creators
- Other creators in your niche
- In-house marketing teams

You are being compared, whether you realize it or not.

That comparison usually comes down to four things:

1. Audience relevance
2. Creative execution
3. Risk
4. Cost

Follower count is part of that equation, but it is rarely the deciding factor. A creator with a smaller but highly relevant audience and strong execution can outperform a much larger creator who feels generic or misaligned.

This is why niche creators often win deals they "shouldn't" win on paper.

What a brand deal actually includes

A brand deal is not just "post a video and get paid." It is a bundle of decisions that all affect value.

Every deal includes some combination of:

- Deliverables
- Rights
- Timing
- Risk
- Expectations

Creators often focus only on deliverables. Brands care about all of it.

Understanding the different deal types helps you identify what you are actually being asked to do and what you should be compensated for.

The main types of brand deals

Paid integrations

This is the most common sponsorship format.

A paid integration is a sponsored segment inside your normal content. The video, post, or episode exists regardless of the brand. The sponsor is integrated into it.

What changes the value of an integration:

- Where it appears in the content
- How long it runs
- Whether it is scripted or flexible
- How directly it asks for action
- How closely it aligns with your usual content

Integrations work well because they feel native. When done correctly, they do not interrupt the experience. When done poorly, they feel like an ad break.

Your job is to protect the experience while delivering the brand's message.

Dedicated content

Dedicated content is when the entire piece is built around the brand or product.

This can be powerful, but it carries more risk. If the content feels forced, your audience will feel it immediately. Dedicated content should only be accepted when you can genuinely create something that fits your channel and still serves your audience.

If the only way to make it work is to change who you are or what you normally post, it is not worth it.

Product-only collaborations

Product-only deals are not inherently bad. They are a tool.

They make sense when:

- You are early and building a portfolio
- You genuinely want the product
- The brand is a good long-term fitYou are setting expectations for future paid work

They stop making sense when:

- You already have proof of performance
- The brand clearly has budgetYou are doing real production work
- The deliverables require significant time

Product does not replace labor. It can offset it, but it does not erase it.

Affiliate and performance-based deals

In affiliate deals, you are paid based on results. Sales, leads, installs, or clicks.

These deals shift risk from the brand to you.

They can work extremely well when:

- The product is already a natural fit
- Your audience trusts you
- The conversion path is simple
- The commission structure is fair

They work poorly when:

- The product is unfamiliar or forced
- The offer is weak
- The brand avoids paying upfront entirely
- You are expected to do heavy creative work for speculative upside

Affiliate deals should be treated as investments, not guarantees.

Hybrid deals

Many real-world deals are hybrids.

For example:

- Lower upfront pay plus affiliate commission
- Product plus a reduced rate
- Paid integration plus performance bonus

Hybrid deals are common because brands want flexibility and creators want upside. They can be great when structured clearly and dangerous when vague.

Clarity matters more than optimism.

User generated content for brands

In these deals, you create content for the brand to use on their own channels or ads. You may not post it yourself at all.

These deals are based on creative skill, not audience size.

This is why creators with small followings can still earn strong income. The value is in your ability to make content that feels authentic and performs well.

This category is often underpriced by creators because it feels separate from "being an influencer." It is still your time, your likeness, and your work.

Licensing and usage rights

This is where many creators lose money.

When a brand wants to reuse your content beyond the original post, they are buying rights. That includes:

- Reposting on their social channels
- Using it on their website
- Including it in emails
- Running it as an ad

Usage is not automatic. It is a separate value.

If your face, voice, or content is used in paid advertising, that carries more weight than organic reposting. The wider and longer the usage, the more valuable it is.

If usage is not discussed, assume it is not included.

Whitelisting and boosted posts

Sometimes brands want to run ads through your account or boost your post directly.

This means the ad appears to come from you, not the brand.

This can perform extremely well, which is why brands like it. It also attaches your name and credibility to a paid campaign.

This is not a free add-on. It carries risk and should be priced accordingly.

Exclusivity

Exclusivity means you agree not to work with competitors for a certain period of time.

Exclusivity limits your future opportunities. Because of that, it has value.

If a brand wants exclusivity, they are buying access to your category. That should be reflected in the deal.

Short exclusivity may be reasonable. Long or vague exclusivity is usually not.

Retainers and ongoing partnerships

Retainers are recurring agreements where a brand pays you monthly for a defined set of deliverables.

These are ideal because:

- Income is predictable
- Expectations are clear

- Relationships deepen
- Negotiations happen less often

Retainers usually come after a successful one-off campaign. They are built on trust and performance, not cold pitches.

Why brands always ask for "just one more thing"

Brands are not trying to scam you most of the time. They are trying to maximize value within a fixed budget.

This is why you will hear:

- "Can we also get this on Instagram?"
- "Can you add a pinned comment?"
- "Can we use this for ads too?"
- "Can you send the raw files?"

Each request sounds small. Together, they add up.

Understanding deal types helps you spot when a deal is expanding without compensation. You do not need to say no to everything. You need to know what you are giving away.

Choosing the right deal for your stage

Not every deal type makes sense at every stage.

Early creators should prioritize:

- Portfolio building
- Proof of execution
- Learning brand communication

Growing creators should prioritize:

- Paid integrations
- Clear boundaries
- Audience alignment

Established creators should prioritize:

- Usage rights
- Retainers
- Long-term partnerships
- Protecting audience trust

The goal is not to take every deal. The goal is to take the right ones.

Chapter takeaway

A brand deal is not one thing. It is a spectrum of arrangements that trade creative work, audience trust, and rights for compensation.

If you understand what type of deal you are in, you gain leverage. If you do not, you will almost always give away more than you realize.

Before moving on, ask yourself:

- Which deal types am I currently accepting?
- Which ones make sense for my stage?
- Which ones have I been undervaluing?

In the next chapter, we will talk about when you can start charging and how creators move from free to paid without burning bridges or sabotaging future income.

2

When You Can Start Charging and How Creators Actually Transition to Paid Deals

One of the most common questions creators ask is, "When can I start charging brands?"

The uncomfortable answer is that there is no universal threshold. No follower count. No view minimum. No magic milestone where brands suddenly take you seriously.

Creators who wait for permission usually wait too long.

Creators who charge too early usually do it poorly.

The difference is not size. It is readiness.

Why follower count is the wrong metric

Follower count is visible, which is why people fixate on it. It is also one of the least reliable indicators of value.

Brands care far more about:

- Who your audience actually is
- How they behave
- Whether they trust you
- Whether you can deliver consistently

A creator with 5,000 highly engaged followers in a specific niche can be more valuable than a creator with 500,000 passive followers who scroll past everything.

This is why creators with "small" audiences sometimes land real deals while larger creators get ignored or lowballed.

The three things brands pay for

Before you charge anyone, you need to understand what brands are buying. It is almost always one or more of the following:

1. **Access**: Direct access to a specific audience they care about.
2. **Execution**: The ability to create content that feels natural and performs.
3. **Reliability**: Confidence that you will deliver on time,

communicate clearly, and not cause problems.

If you can clearly offer even one of these, you can charge. If you can offer all three, you are already late.

Readiness is about proof, not popularity

Charging is less about your numbers and more about your proof.

Proof can look like:

- Consistent content quality
- Repeat viewers or commenters
- Strong audience retention
- Past collaborations, paid or unpaid
- Affiliate performance
- Clear niche alignment

Brands are risk-averse. Proof reduces risk.

This is why early deals often start small. They are tests. Your job is not to squeeze every dollar out of your first paid deal. Your job is to prove you are worth rebooking.

The real path from free to paid

Most creators imagine the path looks like this:

Free → Paid → Bigger Paid → Huge Paid

In reality, it usually looks like this:

Organic content → Affiliate content → Product-only → Paid test → Repeat paid → Retainer

Each step builds leverage.

Skipping steps does not make you advanced. It makes you fragile.

Using product-only deals strategically

Product-only deals get a bad reputation because creators stay in them too long.

Early on, they serve a purpose:

- You learn how brands communicate
- You learn approval processes
- You build a portfolio
- You test how your audience reacts

The mistake is treating them as equal to paid work.

If a product-only deal requires:

- Custom scripting

- Multiple revisions
- Specific posting windows
- Usage rights

Then it is no longer "just a product." It is unpaid labor.

Use product-only deals to build leverage, not as your default.

Setting expectations early

One of the most important things you can do early is signal that free is temporary.

You do this by saying things like: "Happy to do this as a product-only collaboration for now. My standard partnerships are paid." "This works as a test. If it performs well, I'd love to discuss a paid campaign next time."

This frames the relationship correctly from the beginning.

If a brand disappears when payment is mentioned, that is information, not rejection.

The moment you should start charging

You should start charging when at least one of these is true:

- Brands are asking for deliverables with clear expectations

- You are spending real time producing sponsored content
- Your audience is responding positively to integrations
- You have any form of performance proof

Waiting until you feel "big enough" is usually just fear.

Charging poorly can be fixed. Training brands to expect free work is harder to undo.

How much to charge at the beginning

Early paid deals are not about optimization. They are about momentum.

Your first paid deal does not need to be perfect. It needs to:

- Respect your time
- Feel fair
- Set a baseline

It is normal for early rates to feel slightly uncomfortable. If it feels too easy, you are probably undercharging.

At the same time, do not anchor yourself to your first rate forever. Rates change as your leverage grows.

Handling brands that want free work "for exposure"

This request rarely comes from brands that matter.

If a brand truly believes you provide value, they budget for it. Exposure is not a currency you can deposit.

A simple response: "Thanks for reaching out. At this stage, I'm only taking paid partnerships or affiliate-based collaborations."

No justification required.

The fear of scaring brands away

Creators worry that charging will scare brands away. Sometimes it does.

That is not a failure. That is filtering.

Brands that disappear when money is mentioned were never serious partners. They were shopping for free labor.

You are not building a list of brands who will work with you at any cost. You are building a list of brands who value what you do.

When brands suddenly stop responding

This is normal.

Brands ghost for many reasons:

- Budget changed
- Campaign canceled
- Internal delays
- They chose someone else

Silence is not always rejection. Follow up once or twice, then move on.

Do not lower your rate out of panic.

Charging brands you already worked with for free

This is the hardest transition emotionally.

Some brands will understand immediately. Some will not.

When they do not, it usually sounds like: "We've never paid for this before."

Your response is simple: "That worked at the time. My partnerships are structured differently now."

You do not owe discounts for history. You can offer them, but they are optional.

Chapter takeaway

Charging is not about being "ready" in the abstract. It is about reducing risk for the brand and respecting your own time.

If you can deliver value, communicate clearly, and meet expectations, you can charge.

If you wait until you feel confident, you will wait longer than necessary.

In the next chapter, we will talk about pricing itself. Not just numbers, but how creators decide rates, why CPM thinking breaks down, and how to stop guessing.

3

How to Price Yourself Without Guessing

Pricing is where most creators lose money, confidence, or both. Not because they are lazy or uninformed, but because pricing sits at the intersection of value, leverage, psychology, and fear.

Creators want a number.

Brands want a justification.

Neither side actually knows the "correct" answer.

The goal of this chapter is not to give you a magic formula. It is to give you a system that lets you price consistently, defend your rates calmly, and adjust without panic.

Why most pricing advice is useless

If you have searched for pricing advice online, you have probably seen:

- CPM charts
- "Charge $X per 1,000 views"
- Rate calculators
- Spreadsheets that pretend to be science

These tools are not evil. They are incomplete.

They reduce pricing to math, when in reality pricing is about leverage and risk. CPM can explain part of a deal, but it cannot explain why two creators with similar views are paid radically different amounts.

If pricing were purely mathematical, brands would never negotiate.

What your rate actually represents

Your rate is not just payment for posting content.

Your rate represents:

- Your time and effort
- Your creative skill
- Your audience's attention

- Your audience's trust
- The risk you take attaching your name to a brand
- The opportunity cost of saying no to other deals

Once you see pricing as a bundle of value instead of a number, negotiations stop feeling personal.

The three layers of pricing

Every deal has three pricing layers, whether you name them or not.

Layer one: the base deliverable

This is the core thing you are creating.

- A video
- A post
- A short-form clip
- A UGC asset

This is the foundation. It covers production and posting.

Layer two: amplification and distribution

This includes:

- Posting on multiple platforms

- Pinning comments
- Adding links or CTAs
- Timing posts around launches

These increase reach and performance. They increase value.

Layer three: rights and restrictions

This includes:

- Usage rights
- Paid ads usage
- Whitelisting
- Exclusivity
- Category restrictions

This layer is where many creators accidentally give away the most value.

Base rates: your internal pricing anchor

You should have internal base rates for common deliverables. These do not need to be public. They exist so you are not inventing numbers on the fly.

Examples:

- YouTube integration

- Dedicated YouTube video
- Short-form video
- Story set
- UGC video

Your base rate should cover:

- Time spent planning
- Time spent filming
- Time spent editing
- Communication and revisions
- Posting and follow-through

If your base rate does not respect your time, nothing else matters.

Why CPM thinking breaks down

Brands often talk in CPM terms because they are used to buying ads.

CPM thinking assumes:

- Views are guaranteed
- Attention is equal
- Context does not matter

None of those are true in creator content.

A creator video is not a banner ad. It carries personality, trust, and narrative. A brand is not just buying impressions. They are borrowing credibility.

When a brand uses CPM language, they are not insulting you. They are anchoring the conversation to what they understand.

Your job is to shift the frame.

How to respond to CPM-based offers

If a brand says: "We pay $20 CPM."

You do not argue math. You reframe value.

You say something like: "I price based on deliverables, production, and the rights included. If you want to work within that budget, I can suggest a package that makes sense."

This keeps the conversation collaborative instead of defensive.

Add-ons are not greedy, they are honest

Creators often feel awkward charging for add-ons because each one seems small.

That discomfort costs money.

Add-ons exist because:

- They add workload
- They add risk
- They limit future opportunities

Common add-ons that should be priced separately:

- Extra platforms
- Raw footage delivery
- Additional revision rounds
- Tight deadlines
- Usage beyond organic posting
- Paid ads usage
- Whitelisting
- Exclusivity

If a brand wants more, they pay more. That is not greed. That is clarity.

Usage rights: the most misunderstood pricing lever

If a brand wants to reuse your content, they are extending its life and reach beyond the original deal.

Questions that affect usage pricing:

- Where will it be used?

- For how long?
- Organic only or paid?
- On which platforms?
- Is your likeness central to the ad?

Short, organic reposting may be a small add-on. Paid advertising usage is not.

If your face is running as an ad, you are now part of their media spend.

Whitelisting and boosted posts

Whitelisting allows a brand to run ads through your account or boost your post.

This creates:

- Higher performance
- Stronger perceived authenticity
- Direct association with your brand

It also creates risk.

If the ad performs poorly or the comments turn negative, it reflects on you. That risk should be compensated.

Whitelisting is not included by default.

Exclusivity and opportunity cost

Exclusivity prevents you from working with competitors.

The longer and broader the exclusivity, the higher the opportunity cost.

Exclusivity should be priced based on:

- Category
- Duration
- Scope

Short exclusivity in a narrow category may be reasonable. Long exclusivity across an entire industry usually is not.

If a brand wants to lock you out of future income, they need to pay for it.

Discounting without devaluing yourself

Discounts are not evil. Random discounts are.

Discounts should be intentional:

- Bundle discounts
- Long-term partnership discounts
- First-time test discounts

Avoid "panic discounts" driven by fear of losing the deal.

If you discount, say why: "I'm happy to offer this rate for an initial test campaign."

This preserves your future leverage.

The psychology of pricing conversations

Pricing feels personal because rejection feels personal.

Brands expect negotiation. Silence after you send a rate is normal. It does not mean you priced incorrectly.

Your calm matters more than your number.

If you sound uncertain, brands will push. If you sound grounded, brands adjust.

When to say no

You should say no when:

- The brand is a poor audience fit
- The deal requires excessive work for low pay
- The contract removes too much control
- The brand disrespects your time

Saying no protects your future pricing more than saying yes to everything.

Chapter takeaway

Pricing is not about guessing the perfect number. It is about understanding what you are selling and why it matters.

Have base rates. Price add-ons. Protect your rights. Stay calm.

In the next chapter, we will build the tool that supports all of this: your media kit, and how to design it so it actually closes instead of just looking nice.

4

Creating a Media Kit That Actually Works

A media kit is not a resume.

It is not a scrapbook.

It is not a flex document.

A media kit has one job: reduce friction so a brand can confidently say yes.

Most media kits fail because they try to impress instead of inform. They overload brands with stats, screenshots, quotes, and fluff while failing to answer the few questions that actually matter.

A good media kit feels obvious. A bad one feels noisy.

Why brands ask for a media kit in the first place

When a brand asks for your media kit, they are not asking because they want homework. They are asking because they need to validate you internally.

Your point of contact often needs to:

- Forward your info to a manager
- Drop it into a slide deck
- Compare you against other creators
- Justify budget spend

Your media kit exists to make that easy.

If your kit answers questions quickly, you look professional.

If it raises questions, you look risky.

The biggest mistake creators make

Creators treat media kits like portfolios.

Brands do not need proof that you are creative. They already saw your content or they would not be talking to you.

What they need is clarity.

Clarity about:

- Who you reach
- Why that audience matters
- What you can deliver
- What working with you is like

Anything that does not serve that purpose is filler.

The mental model for a strong media kit

Think of your media kit as a short sales document, not a profile.

Every page should answer one question:

- Who are you?
- Where do you show up?
- Who do you reach?
- What can you offer?
- Why should we trust you?
- How do we move forward?

If a page does not clearly answer one of those, it does not belong.

Page 1: Who you are

This page sets the tone.

Include:

- A clean photo of yourself
- Your name and brand
- A short, clear description of what you make and who it is for

This is not a biography. Two or three sentences is enough.

A good description tells a brand:

- Your platform
- Your niche
- Your audience type
- Your content style

Example framing: "I create YouTube content focused on desk setups, tech, and home workspaces for creators and professionals."

Simple beats clever.

Page 2: Where you show up

This is where you list your platforms.

Only include platforms you are willing to monetize. Do not list every account you own.

For each platform, include:

- Follower or subscriber count
- Average views or reach
- Posting frequency
- One short line about performance or audience behavior

Brands care more about averages than outliers.

If one platform is your primary channel, make that obvious. Everything else should feel supportive, not equal.

Page 3: Audience snapshot

This page answers the question, "Who would see this?"

Include:

- Top countries
- Age ranges
- Gender split if relevant
- Any standout audience insights

Do not overwhelm this page.

Brands are scanning for alignment, not demographic perfection. A clean snapshot builds confidence.

Page 4: What brands can buy

This is one of the most important pages in the entire kit.

Your job here is not to list everything you are capable of. Your job is to show what you sell most often.

Limit this to a handful of clear offerings, such as:

- YouTube integrations
- Dedicated videos
- Short form content
- User generated content
- Optional add-ons

Each offering should include:

- A short description
- What the brand gets
- Where it runs

You are setting expectations, not locking yourself into rigid packages.

Page 5: Proof without bragging

This page answers the question, "Have other brands trusted you?"

Proof can include:

- Brand logos
- Short case studies
- Performance highlights

Do not overload this page.

Two strong examples are better than ten weak ones.

If you have no paid brand history yet, this page can still exist. Use:

- Organic content performance
- Affiliate results
- Product reviews
- Campaign-style breakdowns

Proof is about credibility, not payment history.

Page 6: Pricing or no pricing

This is a strategic choice.

There is no universally correct answer.

Including rates:

- Filters unserious inquiries
- Reduces lowball offers
- Saves time

Excluding rates:

- Keeps flexibility
- Encourages conversation
- Allows custom pricing

A middle ground works well.

List:

- "Starting at" pricing
- Minimums for certain deliverables
- A note that packages are customized

This signals professionalism without boxing you in.

Page 7: Next steps and contact

This page should remove any confusion about how to proceed.

Include:

- Your preferred contact method
- A clear call to action
- Optional availability notes

Make it easy for someone to forward your kit and say, "Reach out to them."

If your kit is public, be mindful of privacy. A dedicated business email and a secondary contact method are usually enough.

Design matters, but not how you think

A media kit does not need to be flashy.

It needs to be:

- Easy to read
- Consistent with your brand
- Easy to update

Templates are fine. Simple layouts are fine. Overdesigned kits often hurt more than they help.

Choose a format you can maintain.

If updating your kit feels like a chore, you will not keep it current.

How often to update your media kit

At minimum:

- Update stats every few months
- Update brand logos as new partnerships happen
- Update offerings if your content evolves

If you experience significant growth, update sooner.

Always include the month and year your stats were pulled. That single detail builds trust.

How brands actually use your media kit

Your media kit is rarely read top to bottom.

It is skimmed.

It is forwarded.

It is screenshot.

This is why clarity matters more than creativity.

A good kit helps someone say, "This makes sense."

A bad kit creates hesitation.

Chapter takeaway

A media kit is not about impressing brands. It is about removing doubt.

Clear beats clever. Focus beats variety. Proof beats hype.

When your media kit does its job, pricing conversations get easier, negotiations feel calmer, and deals close faster.

In the next chapter, we will move from preparation to action and break down cold outreach, how to write emails that get replies, and how to stop wasting time pitching the wrong people.

5

Cold Outreach That Actually Gets Replies

Cold outreach is where most creators stall out. Not because it does not work, but because it is done poorly, inconsistently, or with the wrong expectations.

Cold outreach is not about convincing brands to like you.

It is about starting a conversation with the right person at the right time.

When done correctly, it is one of the fastest ways to land sponsorships. When done incorrectly, it feels like screaming into the void.

Why most cold outreach fails

Cold outreach usually fails for one of four reasons:

1. The message is too long
2. The message is too vague
3. The message is sent to the wrong person
4. The creator treats silence as rejection

Most creators try to solve this by sending more emails. That only amplifies the problem.

The fix is not volume. It is precision.

What cold outreach is actually for

Cold outreach is not meant to close a deal.

Its only job is to earn a reply.

That reply can be:

- "Tell me more"
- "What are your rates?"
- "Looping in my colleague"
- "Not a fit right now"

All of those are wins.

Silence is the only true loss.

Once you get a reply, the dynamic changes. You are no longer cold. You are now in a conversation.

The mindset shift creators need

Creators approach cold outreach like they are asking for permission.

Brands read cold outreach like they are scanning for relevance.

Your job is not to pitch everything you can do. Your job is to signal quickly that:

- You understand their brand
- You understand your audience
- There is a logical overlap worth exploring

If that overlap is clear, the conversation continues.

Who you should be reaching out to

Cold outreach works best when you target brands that already spend money on marketing.

Good signs:

- They run ads
- They work with creators already
- They have an active social presence
- They sell products or services with margin

Cold outreach to brands that do not market is almost always wasted effort.

Timing matters more than creators think

Brands do not buy sponsorships continuously. They buy around:

- Product launches
- Sales cycles
- Seasonal pushes
- Campaign planning windows

If you email a brand when nothing is happening internally, silence is likely.

This is why follow-ups matter. Not because your first email was bad, but because timing was wrong.

The anatomy of a cold email that works

A strong cold email is short, specific, and easy to understand.

It answers five things quickly:

- Who you are
- What you do
- Why this brand makes sense
- What you are proposing
- What the next step is

Anything beyond that belongs in a follow-up or a call.

Subject lines that get opened

Your subject line should look like it was written by a human, not a campaign tool.

Effective patterns:

- Brand name plus your name
- Platform specific partnerships
- Simple collaboration framing

Examples:

- Brand X Matt Philie

- YouTube partnership idea
- Short form content idea for Brand

Avoid:

- All caps
- Emojis
- Buzzwords
- Anything that sounds automated

The cold email structure

Opening

Identify yourself and your platform in one sentence.

This establishes context immediately.

Example: "My name is Matt Philie. I create YouTube content focused on tech and desk setups."

Relevance

Show why this brand is a fit.

This is where most creators fail by being generic.

Bad: "I think your brand is great and would love to work together."

Better: "I recently featured desk lighting solutions, and your product fits directly into the setups my audience asks about."

This shows intent, not flattery.

The idea

Propose one clear concept.

Do not list five options. Do not pitch your entire inventory.

Example: "I'd like to explore a YouTube integration that highlights how your product fits into a real-world setup rather than a standalone review."

Specific beats flexible.

The ask

Invite conversation, not commitment.

Example: "If this sounds interesting, I can share package options and timing."

This feels low pressure while moving forward.

Close

Provide links and contact details.

Make it easy for them to validate you quickly.

A complete cold email example

Subject: Brand X Matt Philie (YouTube)

Hi [Name],

My name is Matt Philie. I create YouTube content around desk setups and tech for creators and home offices.

I had an idea for a YouTube integration that shows how Brand X fits naturally into a real workspace setup rather than a standalone product mention.

If this is something you are exploring, I'd be happy to share a few package options and timing.

Here's my channel and a recent example:

[Channel link]

[Example link]

Thanks,

Matt

That is enough. Anything longer usually hurts response rates.

Follow-ups are not annoying, they are necessary

Most replies come from follow-ups, not first emails.

Brands are busy. Emails get buried.

A simple follow-up after a few business days is expected.

Example: "Hi [Name], just bumping this in case it got buried. Happy to share details if it's a fit."

A second follow-up a week later is also reasonable.

If there is still no response, move on.

Silence is not personal.

When to stop following up

Two follow-ups is usually enough.

If you hear nothing after that, either:

- The timing is wrong
- The contact is wrong

- The brand is not interested

All three are outside your control.

Do not chase. Do not discount. Do not send a novel explaining yourself.

Phone calls and alternative contact methods

Email is not the only option, but it is the safest starting point.

For some brands:

- A phone call can get you routed to the right department
- A social DM can surface the correct contact
- A website chat can provide a direct email

Use these sparingly and professionally.

Your goal is access, not persistence theater.

Why personalization matters more than volume

Sending ten well researched emails beats sending one hundred generic ones.

Personalization does not mean writing an essay. It means one sentence that could not be copied and pasted.

That one sentence is often what gets you a reply.

The emotional side of cold outreach

Rejection stings. Silence feels worse.

The mistake creators make is tying outreach results to self worth.

Cold outreach is a numbers game layered on timing and relevance. Even strong pitches get ignored. Even weak pitches sometimes land.

Detach your ego from the outcome.

Chapter takeaway

Cold outreach is not about convincing brands to sponsor you. It is about starting conversations with brands that already make sense.

Be short. Be specific. Follow up. Move on.

In the next chapter, we will focus on what happens after outreach works. How to find the right contact, avoid dead ends, and stop pitching into generic inboxes.

6

Finding the Right Contact Without Wasting Time

Cold outreach only works if it reaches the right person. A strong email sent to the wrong inbox is still a wasted effort.

Most creators assume silence means rejection. More often, it means the message never reached someone who could act on it.

This chapter is about access. Not hacks. Not shortcuts. Just understanding how companies are structured and how to navigate them without burning energy.

Why the "contact us" page rarely works

Generic inboxes exist to filter, not route.

Addresses like:

- info@

- hello@
- support@
- contact@

are designed to catch customers, not partnership inquiries.

When your email lands there, it is usually handled by:

- Customer support
- Interns
- Automated systems

None of those people control marketing budgets.

This does not mean those inboxes are useless. It means they should be a last resort, not your first move.

Who actually handles partnerships

At most companies, partnerships are handled by:

- Influencer marketing managers
- Brand marketing managers
- Social media managers
- Growth marketing teams
- External agencies

Your job is not to guess titles perfectly. Your job is to reach someone who understands marketing and has the authority to pass your message forward.

If your email reaches someone who can forward it internally, that is often enough.

Start with the company's own signals

Before hunting emails, look at how the brand already works.

Ask yourself:

- Do they work with creators?
- Are they tagged in sponsored posts?
- Do they run influencer campaigns?
- Do they repost creator content?

If the answer is yes, someone is managing that.

Scroll through:

- Their social media
- Tagged posts
- Paid ads
- Creator mentions

Often, creators thank or tag the brand's campaign team. Those names are clues.

Use the website strategically

A brand's website usually contains more than one point of entry.

Check:

- Press or media pages
- Careers pages
- Blog author bios
- Footer links

Press pages often list a media or PR contact. While PR is not the same as influencer marketing, PR teams know where to route inquiries.

Careers pages can reveal titles and departments, which helps you search more accurately elsewhere.

Social platforms as research tools

LinkedIn is one of the most underused tools for creators.

Search the company name and look for:

- Influencer marketing
- Partnerships
- Social media
- Brand marketing

You do not need to connect with everyone. You need names.

Once you have names, you can often infer email formats.

Email format inference

Many companies use predictable email formats:

- firstname@company.com
- firstname.lastname@company.com
- firstinitiallastname@company.com

If you find one confirmed email on the site, you can often extrapolate.

This is not guaranteed, but it works more often than people expect.

When in doubt, send one email. Do not blast multiple guessed emails.

Agencies: the hidden gatekeepers

Many brands outsource creator campaigns to agencies.

If a brand's influencer campaigns feel polished and consistent, there is often an agency involved.

Signs of agency involvement:

- Consistent creator briefs
- Similar content across creators
- Coordinated posting schedules

If an agency is involved, your best move may be contacting the agency instead of the brand. Agencies manage multiple brands and are always looking for reliable creators.

Using social DMs professionally

Direct messages can work, but only in specific contexts.

Good use cases:

- Asking who handles partnerships
- Confirming the right contact
- Following up after email

Bad use cases:

- Pitching full campaigns
- Sending media kits
- Negotiating rates

A DM should be short and functional.

Example: "Hi, quick question. Who handles creator partnerships for your brand?"

That is it.

Phone calls are underrated

Calling a company feels intimidating, but it can save hours.

You are not pitching on the phone. You are asking to be routed.

Example: "Hi, could you point me to the person who handles influencer partnerships?"

You may be transferred. You may get a name. Both are wins.

Be polite. Be brief. Respect their time.

When to stop digging

Some companies make it hard to find the right contact because they do not want inquiries.

If you:

- Searched the site
- Checked social platforms
- Looked for agencies
- Tried a reasonable alternative

and still cannot find a contact, move on.

Your time is valuable. Not every brand is worth chasing.

What to do when you reach the wrong person

Sometimes you will email the wrong department. That is normal.

If they reply, thank them and ask to be forwarded.

If they do not reply, do not apologize excessively. Just try a different route next time.

Most internal forwarding happens because someone thought you were professional, not because you begged.

Why politeness matters more than persistence

The creator world is smaller than it feels.

People move between brands and agencies. The person ignoring you today may be hiring you tomorrow at a different company.

Always assume emails can be forwarded.

Professional tone costs nothing and protects your reputation.

Tracking your outreach

If you do cold outreach seriously, track it.

You do not need complex software. A simple spreadsheet works.

Track:

- Brand
- Contact name
- Email
- Date sent
- Follow-up status
- Outcome

This prevents duplicate emails and helps you improve over time.

Chapter takeaway

Finding the right contact is about understanding how companies work, not brute force.

Generic inboxes filter you out. Specific people move things forward.

If you can consistently reach the right person, your outreach success rate will improve dramatically without sending more emails.

In the next chapter, we will talk about what happens once brands reply. How to handle inbound interest, what questions to ask, how to spot red flags, and how to avoid giving away leverage too early.

7

Handling Inbound Emails and Qualifying Brand Interest

Inbound emails feel like validation. A brand found you, reached out, and wants to work together. That excitement is exactly why creators make their biggest mistakes here.

Inbound interest does not mean the brand is serious.

Inbound interest does not mean the brand has budget.

Inbound interest does not mean the deal will be fair.

Your job is not to say yes quickly. Your job is to slow the conversation down, gather information, and protect your leverage.

Why inbound deals still need structure

When a brand emails you first, the power dynamic shifts slightly in your favor. They chose you. That matters.

Many creators accidentally give that leverage away by:

- Sending rates immediately
- Overexplaining their value
- Agreeing to unclear deliverables
- Accepting vague terms

Inbound does not mean easier. It means different.

The most common inbound email types

Most inbound emails fall into one of these categories:

1. Exploratory outreach "We love your content and would love to collaborate."
2. Product seeding "We'd like to send you a product to try."
3. Budgeted campaigns "We're planning a campaign and would like your rates."
4. Agency casting calls "Our client is looking for creators in your niche."

Each type requires a different response.

Never send your rate as the first reply

This is one of the most important rules in this book.

If you send your rate before understanding the scope, you lose control of the conversation.

Instead, your first response should gather information.

You want to know:

- What platform?
- What deliverables?
- What timeline?
- What usage?
- What budget range?
- Is this paid, product-only, or hybrid?

Without this, any number you send is a guess.

A strong first reply template

Here is a simple response that works across most inbound inquiries:

"Thanks for reaching out. Happy to explore this. Could you share more details on the deliverables, platforms, timeline, and whether this is a paid campaign or product-based? Once I have that, I can suggest options."

This does three things:

- Shows interest
- Signals professionalism
- Forces clarity

How to identify serious brands quickly

Serious brands can answer basic questions.

If a brand:

- Avoids discussing budget
- Keeps deliverables vague
- Pushes for free work immediately
- Rushes you without details

That is a red flag.

Lack of clarity is often intentional.

Product seeding emails: how to respond

Product seeding can be legitimate or lazy.

A good response: "Happy to receive the product. To set expectations, my standard partnerships are paid. If this performs well,

I'd be open to discussing a paid campaign."

This keeps the door open without committing to free labor.

If they push for guaranteed posting in exchange for product, that is no longer seeding. That is a product-only deal.

Treat it accordingly.

Agencies vs brands

Agency emails often feel impersonal. That is normal.

Agencies manage volume. They care about:

- Reliability
- Turnaround time
- Ease of communication

If you are professional and responsive, agencies remember you.

Never assume agencies are low budget. Many control large spends. Treat them seriously.

Budget questions are not rude

Creators hesitate to ask about budget because they fear sounding greedy.

Brands expect budget discussions.

If you need to ask directly, do it neutrally: "Do you have a budget range in mind for this campaign?"

This saves time for everyone.

How to handle low offers

Low offers are not insults. They are anchors.

You can respond by:

- Countering with a higher rate
- Reducing scope
- Offering alternatives

Example: "That budget is lower than my standard rate for this scope. If helpful, I can suggest a scaled-down option that fits."

This keeps the conversation alive without devaluing yourself.

When to walk away

Walk away when:

- The brand disrespects boundaries
- The contract is unreasonable
- The workload is excessive for the pay
- The brand is a poor fit for your audience

Walking away early saves more time than fixing bad deals later.

Managing multiple inbound conversations

As inbound increases, organization matters.

Use:

- Labels or folders in your email
- A simple CRM or spreadsheet
- Calendar reminders for follow-ups

Professionalism is remembered.

Why speed matters, but rushing does not

Responding quickly is good. Responding hastily is not.

Timely replies show reliability. Thoughtful replies protect leverage.

You do not need to reply instantly. You need to reply clearly.

Chapter takeaway

Inbound interest is an opportunity, not a guarantee.

Slow down. Ask questions. Gather details. Protect your position.

The creators who earn consistently are not the ones who say yes the fastest. They are the ones who qualify opportunities properly.

In the next chapter, we will cover agreements, contracts, usage rights, and how to avoid signing something that quietly takes more than you realize.

8

Agreements, Contracts, and Protecting Yourself

This is the chapter most creators skip until something goes wrong.

Contracts feel boring. Legal language feels intimidating. When a brand sends paperwork, the temptation is to skim, sign, and move on so the deal can "officially" start.

That instinct is how creators get burned.

You do not need to become a lawyer. You do need to understand what you are agreeing to and where creators quietly give away leverage, rights, or future income.

AGREEMENTS, CONTRACTS, AND PROTECTING YOURSELF

Why contracts exist in the first place

A contract is not there to protect feelings. It exists to define expectations and reduce risk.

For brands, contracts protect:

- Their money
- Their messaging
- Their timelines
- Their legal exposure

For you, contracts protect:

- Your time
- Your work
- Your rights
- Your payment

When a contract is vague, both sides lose. When a contract is one-sided, only one side wins.

Not every agreement looks like a contract

Creators often think "contract" means a 20-page legal document.

In reality, agreements can look like:

- Formal contracts
- Statements of work
- Email agreements
- Platform-generated terms
- Click-to-sign documents

If expectations are written down and agreed to, it is an agreement.

Do not assume something is harmless because it looks simple.

When you should involve a lawyer

You do not need a lawyer for every deal.

You should strongly consider one when:

- The agreement is long or complex
- There is exclusivity
- There is paid advertising usage
- There is perpetual usage language
- There are penalties or clawbacks
- The deal value is significant

Think of legal review as insurance. It costs something, but it prevents much bigger losses.

The clauses creators need to understand

You do not need to understand every word in a contract. You do need to understand the clauses that matter most.

Deliverables

This section defines what you are actually required to do.

Check for:

- Platform
- Format
- Length
- Posting requirements
- Deadlines
- Approval steps

If deliverables are vague, expect scope creep.

If it says "including but not limited to," that is a red flag. Everything should be specific.

Timeline and approvals

Look for:

- When drafts are dueHow many revision rounds are allowed
- How long the brand has to review
- What happens if they delay approval

Without limits, approvals can drag on indefinitely.

A good contract defines:

- Review windows
- Revision caps
- What counts as a valid revision

Payment terms

This section matters more than the number.

Check for:

- Total amount
- Payment schedule
- Deposit requirements
- Net termsPayment method

Common traps:

- Net 60 or Net 90 without discussion
- Payment contingent on posting only

- Payment contingent on performance

If payment is delayed, you are effectively financing the campaign.

Usage rights

Usage clauses are where creators lose the most value.

Look for:

- Where content can be used
- For how long
- On which platforms
- Organic versus paid usage

Language like "in perpetuity" or "worldwide, unlimited usage" should never be ignored.

If usage is broad, compensation should reflect that.

Paid advertising and whitelisting

Paid ads are not the same as reposting.

If the brand can run your content as an ad:

- You are endorsing them at scale
- Your likeness becomes part of their media buy
- Your reputation is attached to performance

This should be clearly defined and compensated.

Exclusivity and non-competes

Exclusivity limits your future earning potential.

Check for:

- Category definitions
- Duration
- Scope

Vague exclusivity like "similar products" can block entire industries.

If exclusivity exists, it should be narrow and time-bound.

Ownership and intellectual property

In most creator deals:

- You create the content
- The brand licenses usage

Be cautious of language that transfers ownership entirely.

Selling ownership is not inherently wrong. It just needs to be priced accordingly.

Termination and kill fees

Kill fees protect you if a campaign is canceled after work begins.

Look for:

- Cancellation rights
- Compensation if the project ends early
- What happens if you already delivered work

Without a kill fee, you carry all the risk.

Red flags to watch for

Some language should make you pause immediately:

- "In perpetuity"
- "Including but not limited to"
- "At brand's sole discretion"
- "Without additional compensation"
- "All media now known or later developed"

These phrases are not automatically deal-breakers, but they require scrutiny.

Negotiating contracts without drama

Negotiation does not mean confrontation.

A professional approach: "I'm good with most of this. I do have a few questions around usage and revisions. Can we adjust those sections?"

Most brands expect revisions. Silence helps no one.

What to do if there is no contract

Some brands do not provide contracts, especially smaller ones.

If there is no contract:

- Clarify deliverables in writing
- Confirm payment terms
- Confirm usage expectations
- Save all communication

Email agreements still matter.

Never rely on trust alone

Most brands are not malicious. That does not mean mistakes will not happen.

Protect yourself with clarity, not suspicion.

A clear agreement helps good brands be good partners.

Chapter takeaway

Contracts are not there to scare you. They are there to define the deal.

Read everything. Question anything unclear. Negotiate where it matters.

Protecting yourself is not being difficult. It is being professional.

In the next chapter, we will talk about getting paid, deposits, invoicing, late payments, and how to avoid doing work without compensation.

9

Getting Paid Without Chasing

Getting a brand deal is exciting. Getting paid for it should be boring.

If payment feels stressful, unclear, or delayed, something upstream was handled poorly. Most payment problems are not accidents. They are the result of vague terms, weak boundaries, or assumptions made too early.

This chapter is about turning payment into a process instead of a hope.

Why creators get paid late

Late payment is usually blamed on brands being careless or shady. Sometimes that's true. Most of the time, it's structural.

Common causes:

- Payment terms were never clearly agreed to
- Invoicing was delayed or incorrect
- Payment was tied to posting or performance
- The creator was not treated like a vendor
- The brand's finance team was never looped in

You cannot fix all of these after the fact. You can prevent most of them before work starts.

You are a vendor, not a favor

One mental shift solves many payment issues.

You are not "getting paid by a brand."

You are providing a service to a client.

Once you frame yourself as a vendor:

- Invoicing becomes normal
- Deposits make sense
- Payment timelines matter
- Late payments get followed up on professionally

Brands are used to paying vendors. Problems arise when creators behave like exceptions.

Always confirm payment terms before work begins

Before you film, edit, or post anything, you should know:

- How much you are being paid
- When you are being paid
- How you are being paid
- What triggers payment

If any of those are unclear, stop.

Excitement is not a substitute for clarity.

Deposits: when and why they matter

Deposits protect you from wasted effort.

They matter most when:

- The project requires significant prep
- The deliverables are custom
- The timeline is long
- The brand is new to you

A common structure:

- 50 percent upfront
- 50 percent upon approval or posting

Some brands will push back. That is not automatically a red flag. Large companies often have rigid payment systems.

If a deposit is not possible, be extra strict about terms.

Net terms explained

Net terms define how long a brand has to pay after invoicing.

Common examples:

- Net 15
- Net 30
- Net 45
- Net 60

Longer terms favor the brand, not you.

If a brand insists on long net terms:

- Price accordingly
- Set reminders
- Confirm invoicing requirements early

Late payment is often caused by invoices submitted incorrectly or to the wrong system.

Invoicing correctly matters more than creators realize

Brands do not pay emails. They pay invoices.

Before invoicing, ask:

- Do you need a PO number?
- Is there a specific invoicing portal?
- Who should receive the invoice?
- Are there formatting requirements?

One missing detail can delay payment by weeks.

What to include on your invoice

At minimum:

- Your legal name or business name
- Contact information
- Invoice number
- Invoice date
- Description of services
- Amount due
- Payment terms
- Payment method

Clear invoices reduce back-and-forth and speed up processing.

When payment is tied to posting

Some deals pay after content goes live. This is common.

If payment is post-publication:

- Make sure posting dates are clear
- Confirm approval requirements
- Do not post before approval if payment depends on it

Never agree to payment that depends on performance metrics unless explicitly structured that way.

Views are not guaranteed.

Kill fees and canceled campaigns

Campaigns get canceled. Budgets change. Strategies shift.

This is why kill fees exist.

A kill fee ensures you are compensated if:

- The campaign is canceled after work begins
- The brand delays indefinitely
- The project is paused without resolution

Even partial compensation is better than none.

How to follow up on late payments professionally

Late payments happen even with good brands.

A professional follow-up: "Hi, just checking on the status of invoice #123. Let me know if you need anything from me to process payment."

This is neutral and effective.

Avoid emotional language. Avoid threats. Be persistent and calm.

Escalation without burning bridges

If payment is significantly late:

- Loop in your original contact
- Ask if there is a finance contact
- Reference agreed terms
- Document everything

Escalation does not mean aggression. It means clarity.

When to stop working with a brand

A brand that:

- Repeatedly pays late
- Avoids communication
- Ignores agreed terms

is not worth long-term partnership.

Reliability matters as much as pay rate.

Chapter Takeaway

Getting paid should be predictable, not stressful.

Treat yourself like a vendor. Confirm terms early. Invoice correctly. Follow up professionally.

In the next chapter, we will cover delivering content, approvals, revisions, and how to avoid endless feedback loops that eat your time.

10

Delivering Content Without Losing Control

Delivering sponsored content is where good deals turn bad if you are not careful. Most problems do not come from malicious brands. They come from unclear expectations, unlimited feedback loops, and creators trying too hard to please.

Your goal is not to hand over control.

Your goal is to collaborate while protecting your time, voice, and boundaries.

Professional delivery is what separates creators who get rebooked from creators who get avoided.

Why delivery matters more than people think

Brands remember two things long after a campaign ends:

- How the content performed
- How working with you felt

Performance matters. Experience matters more.

A smooth delivery process builds trust. A chaotic one creates friction even if the results are decent.

The creator mistake that causes most issues

Creators assume approval means creative ownership transfers to the brand.

It does not.

Approval exists to ensure:

- Required talking points are included
- Brand safety standards are met
- Legal requirements are satisfied

Approval is not meant to rewrite your content or override your style.

If you treat approval like creative surrender, you invite problems.

Set expectations before you create anything

Before you film or design anything, confirm:

- What needs approval
- How many revision rounds are included
- What counts as a valid revision
- How long the brand has to review

If this is not defined, revisions expand until you stop responding.

Boundaries upfront feel professional. Boundaries later feel defensive.

Script approval vs content approval

Not all projects require script approval.

Script approval makes sense when:

- The brand is regulated
- Messaging must be precise
- Legal claims are involved

Script approval often causes delays. Build that into timelines.

For looser integrations, outline approval may be enough. This keeps things moving without micromanagement.

The revision trap

Unlimited revisions benefit no one.

Common revision creep looks like:

- Small wording tweaks
- Tone changes
- New talking points
- Creative direction shifts

One round of revisions is normal. Two is generous. More than that should trigger a conversation.

Your time is part of the cost.

How to handle revision requests professionally

When revisions are reasonable, make them quickly.

When revisions exceed scope, respond calmly: "Happy to help. This goes beyond the agreed revision scope. Let me know if you'd like to proceed with an additional round."

This reframes the request as a choice, not a demand.

Watermarking and trust

Some creators watermark drafts out of fear.

Watermarks can signal distrust and create tension. A solid agreement is better protection.

If you do watermark, keep it subtle and temporary.

Trust is built through clarity, not defensive tactics.

File delivery and organization

Messy delivery makes you look unreliable.

Best practices:

- Use organized folders
- Label files clearly
- Include final and backup versions
- Keep everything accessible

If the brand needs something later, you can provide it without scrambling.

Platform-specific approvals

Some platforms require unique handling.

For long-form video:

- Unlisted uploads are common
- Clarify if full video review is required
- Confirm what can and cannot be changed

For short-form:

- Preview files are often sufficient
- Clarify caption and hashtag approval

Do not assume one platform's process applies to another.

Posting without approval is risky

Unless explicitly agreed otherwise, do not post before approval.

Posting early can:

- Delay payment
- Create disputes
- Trigger takedown requests

Approval protects both sides.

Protecting your voice

Your audience follows you, not the brand.

If requested changes would:

- Misrepresent your opinion
- Damage trust
- Feel inauthentic

You are allowed to push back.

A simple response: "This change doesn't align with how I normally speak to my audience. I can adjust within my style if that works."

Most brands respect this when stated clearly.

Performance anxiety and over-delivery

Creators often over-deliver out of fear.

Over-delivery becomes expectation.

Meet expectations first. Exceed them strategically.

Consistency beats heroics.

After posting: what you owe and what you do not

After content goes live:

- Confirm posting
- Share the live link
- Thank the brand

You do not owe:

- Constant updates
- Performance explanations
- Unpaid additional work

If reporting is required, it should be defined in the agreement.

Chapter takeaway

Delivery is not about control. It is about structure.

Clear expectations prevent conflict. Boundaries protect your time. Professionalism builds long-term value.

In the next chapter, we will focus on what happens after delivery. Reporting results, maintaining relationships, and turning one campaign into many.

11

Reporting Results and Getting Rebooked

Most creators think the deal ends when the content goes live. In reality, that is where the most important part begins.

Brands do not remember every creator they work with. They remember the ones who make their job easier, communicate clearly, and think beyond a single post.

If you want repeat deals, retainers, and long-term relationships, this chapter matters more than almost anything else in this book.

Why reporting is about trust, not numbers

Reporting is not about proving you "did a good job."

Brands already know how the content performed.

Reporting is about signaling professionalism.

When you report results proactively, you show:

- You care about outcomes
- You understand the brand's goals
- You are thinking like a partner, not a one-off vendor

This alone separates you from most creators.

What brands actually care about after a campaign

Creators obsess over views. Brands look at a broader picture.

Depending on the campaign, brands may care about:

- Clicks or conversions
- Engagement quality
- Comments mentioning the brand
- Audience sentiment
- Content reusability
- Ease of collaboration

Not every campaign is about direct sales. Many are about testing, awareness, or creative direction.

Your job is to frame results in context.

When to report results

Timing matters.

Good benchmarks:

- 7 days after posting for early performance
- 30 days after posting for fuller data

Do not report immediately unless requested. Data needs time to stabilize.

If a contract specifies reporting timelines, follow those exactly.

What to include in a post-campaign report

A report does not need to be long.

At minimum, include:

- Link to the content
- Views or reach
- Engagement metrics
- Clicks or conversions if available
- Any standout audience reactions

Screenshots are helpful. Overanalysis is not.

How to frame performance honestly

Not every campaign performs exceptionally.

Do not hide weak performance. Do not overhype average results.

Instead, contextualize:

- How it compares to your typical content
- What worked
- What could be improved next time

Brands value honesty. They do not expect perfection.

Highlighting audience sentiment

Qualitative feedback matters more than creators realize.

If comments include:

- Product questions
- Positive reactions
- Purchase intent
- Tagging friends

Highlight those.

This shows impact beyond raw numbers.

The follow-up message that leads to rebooking

After reporting, send a simple follow-up.

Example: "Thanks again for the opportunity. Happy to build on this if you have upcoming campaigns or want to test additional concepts."

This keeps the door open without pressure.

Asking for feedback (and why it helps)

Asking for feedback feels vulnerable. It is also strategic.

A simple line: "Would love any feedback from your side on how this performed or how the process felt."

This accomplishes two things:

- Shows professionalism
- Gives you insight into how brands evaluate you

Feedback helps you improve and signals maturity.

Turning one-off deals into ongoing partnerships

Retainers rarely come from cold pitches. They come from successful campaigns.

If performance and experience were positive:

- Suggest a follow-up idea
- Propose consistency
- Frame it as easier for the brand

Example: "If it's helpful, I'm open to structuring this as a monthly partnership so you have consistent presence without rebriefing each time."

Brands like predictability.

Timing your rebooking ask

Do not pitch immediately after posting.

Wait until:

- Initial performance is visible
- Reporting has been shared
- The brand has had time to evaluate

A rushed rebooking ask feels transactional. A well-timed one feels natural.

When brands go quiet after a campaign

Silence does not always mean dissatisfaction.

Brands move slowly. Budgets shift. Teams change.

Follow up once after reporting. If there is no response, move on professionally.

Your follow-up exists to remind, not chase.

Building a personal contact list

Over time, you will build relationships with:

- Brand managers
- Agency contacts
- Campaign coordinators

These people change jobs. Brands change strategies.

The relationship is with the person, not just the company.

Maintain contact information and stay polite even when campaigns end.

Why professionalism compounds

One good campaign can lead to:

- Repeat work
- Referrals
- Agency invites
- Long-term contracts

One bad experience can quietly remove you from consideration forever.

Professionalism compounds quietly, just like reputation.

Chapter takeaway

Reporting is not optional if you want longevity.

Clear reporting, honest communication, and thoughtful follow-up turn one campaign into many.

In the next chapter, we will talk about maintaining relationships long-term, setting boundaries, and building a sustainable sponsorship pipeline without burning out or selling out.

12

Maintaining Relationships and Building a Sustainable Pipeline

Landing a brand deal feels like progress. Maintaining relationships is what actually builds a career.

Most creators approach sponsorships as isolated wins. The creators who earn consistently treat them as part of a system. The difference is not talent. It is intention.

This chapter is about turning sporadic deals into a steady pipeline without burning bridges, burning out, or becoming someone your audience no longer trusts.

Why one good relationship matters more than ten cold leads

Cold outreach will always be part of the game. Relationships reduce how often you need it.

One good brand relationship can lead to:

- Repeat campaigns
- Increased budgets
- Long-term retainers
- Referrals to other brands or agencies

Brands talk. Agencies share creators. People move jobs and bring trusted creators with them.

Your goal is not to work with everyone. Your goal is to be remembered.

The post-campaign moment creators waste

Most creators disappear after payment clears.

That is the moment to lean in, not vanish.

A simple follow-up after a campaign ends:

- Thanks them for the opportunity
- Acknowledges the collaboration

- Signals interest in future work

This is not networking theater. It is professionalism.

Relationship maintenance does not mean constant contact

You do not need to check in monthly "just because."

Good relationship maintenance looks like:

- A follow-up after a campaign
- Occasional check-ins around relevant launches
- Sharing ideas that fit the brand
- Being responsive when contacted

Bad relationship maintenance looks like:

- Random DMs
- Forced small talk
- Repeated pitching with no context

Respect people's time.

When and how to re-pitch brands you worked with

Re-pitching is easiest when it is anchored to something real.

Good anchors:

- New product launches
- Seasonal campaigns
- Content that performed well previously
- Growth or format changes on your channel

A re-pitch should feel like a continuation, not a restart.

Example: "Last time we worked together, the integration performed well. I'm planning a similar video next month and thought this could be a strong fit again."

That feels natural. Not desperate.

The difference between partners and transactions

Not every brand becomes a long-term partner. That is fine.

Partners:

- Communicate clearly
- Respect boundaries
- Pay on time
- Value your input

Transactional brands:

- Focus only on deliverables
- Negotiate aggressively every time
- Treat creators as interchangeable

Know which is which and invest your energy accordingly.

Saying no without damaging relationships

Saying no is part of sustainability.

You can say no because:

- The timing is wrong
- The fit is off
- The budget does not work
- You are at capacity

How you say no matters more than the no itself.

A clean no: "Thanks for thinking of me. This isn't the right fit for me right now, but I appreciate the opportunity."

You do not owe explanations.

Boundaries are relationship tools

Boundaries are not walls. They are guardrails.

Clear boundaries:

- Protect your schedule
- Protect your creativity
- Protect your audience trust

When brands know your boundaries, they respect you more, not less.

Inconsistent boundaries confuse people. Consistent boundaries build trust.

Building a pipeline instead of reacting to emails

A sustainable pipeline is proactive, not reactive.

This means:

- Knowing which brands you want to work with
- Knowing which industries fit your audience
- Reaching out with intention
- Following up periodically

If you only respond to inbound, your income will fluctuate.

Simple pipeline habits that work

You do not need complex systems.

Effective habits:

- Keep a list of brands you have worked with
- Track outreach and outcomes
- Note which deals felt good and which did not
- Schedule light follow-ups quarterly or semi-annually

Consistency beats intensity.

Avoiding burnout while working with brands

Burnout does not come from working with brands. It comes from overcommitting and underpricing.

Burnout often shows up when:

- You take too many deals
- You accept poor fits
- You undervalue your time
- You chase money instead of alignment

Saying no is a burnout prevention strategy.

Audience trust is your long-term asset

Your audience is the reason brands work with you. Lose their trust and sponsorships dry up.

Protect trust by:

- Choosing relevant brands
- Disclosing clearly
- Being honest in integrations
- Saying no to bad fits

Short-term money is easy to replace. Trust is not.

The quiet power of consistency

Brands value creators who:

- Show up
- Deliver on time
- Communicate clearly
- Stay professional

You do not need to be flashy. You need to be reliable.

Reliability is rare and valuable.

Chapter takeaway

Sustainability is built on relationships, not one-off wins.

Be professional. Be selective. Be consistent.

In the next chapter, we will talk about the line creators fear crossing. Selling out, staying authentic, and making money without losing yourself or your audience.

13

Making Money Without Selling Out

This is the chapter everyone worries about but few people define clearly.

"Selling out" gets thrown around so casually that it loses meaning. Most of the time, it is used by people who have never tried to build something sustainable.

Making money is not selling out.

Working with brands is not selling out.

Getting paid well is not selling out.

Selling out happens when you abandon your audience, your values, or your standards in exchange for short-term gain.

This chapter is about drawing that line intentionally instead of stumbling over it later.

Why creators fear this more than they should

Creators fear selling out because their audience feels personal.

You are not a faceless company. You are a human with a voice, opinions, and a relationship with viewers. That makes monetization feel vulnerable.

The mistake is assuming authenticity and income are opposites.

They are not.

What actually defines a sell-out

Selling out is not about frequency. It is about alignment.

You are selling out when:

- You promote products you would never use
- You lie or exaggerate for money
- You hide sponsorships
- You change your content purely to attract brands
- You ignore your audience's trust signals

Notice what is missing from that list. Money.

Money is not the issue. Dishonesty is.

The difference between audience-first and brand-first creators

Audience-first creators ask:

- Does this make sense for my viewers?
- Would I be okay recommending this without payment?
- Does this fit naturally into my content?

Brand-first creators ask:

- How much does it pay?
- Can I make it fit?
- Will anyone notice?

Audiences can feel the difference immediately.

Disclosure is not optional, it is protective

Clear disclosure does not hurt trust. Hiding sponsorships does.

Most audiences are reasonable. They understand creators need income.

What they do not tolerate is feeling tricked.

Simple, clear disclosure builds credibility. Over-explaining makes it awkward. Hiding it breaks trust.

Relevance beats payout every time

A smaller, aligned deal often outperforms a larger, mismatched one.

Aligned deals:

- Convert better
- Feel more natural
- Receive less pushback
- Lead to repeat work

Mismatched deals:

- Feel forced
- Trigger negative comments
- Perform poorly
- Hurt future opportunities

Brands notice this too.

Saying no is a long-term strategy

The hardest no is the first one.

After that, it gets easier.

Every no:

- Sharpens your brand
- Protects your audience
- Signals confidence
- Makes future yeses stronger

Saying yes to everything blurs your identity. Saying no defines it.

Handling audience criticism gracefully

No matter what you do, someone will complain.

You do not need to defend every decision.

If criticism is valid:

- Listen
- Adjust
- Learn

If criticism is noise:

- Ignore it
- Stay consistent

Do not let a loud minority dictate your entire strategy.

Why authenticity compounds over time

Creators who stay aligned build trust slowly. Then it snowballs.

Their audience:

- Assumes honesty
- Gives benefit of the doubt
- Engages more deeply
- Supports monetization

This makes brands happier too.

Trust is leverage.

Money as a tool, not a goal

Money gives you:

- Time
- Flexibility
- Creative freedom
- Stability

When money becomes the goal, content suffers.

When money supports the goal, content improves.

This is the balance creators miss.

Building your own rules early

Decide now:

- What categories you will never promote
- What disclosures you will always include
- What minimum standards you have
- What kind of brands excite you

Rules remove indecision later.

The quiet confidence of aligned creators

Aligned creators do not panic about monetization.

They:

- Charge fairly
- Deliver well
- Sleep at night
- Keep their audience

They play the long game.

Chapter takeaway

Selling out is not about money. It is about integrity.

If you protect your audience, communicate honestly, and choose alignment over desperation, monetization becomes sustainable instead of stressful.

In the final chapter, we will wrap everything together. Mindset, systems, mistakes to avoid, and how to move forward with confidence instead of guessing.

14

The Long Game and Final Takeaways

If you take nothing else from this book, take this:

Brand deals are not the goal.

A sustainable creator career is the goal.

Sponsorships are just one tool inside a much bigger system. When you treat them as quick wins, they feel chaotic and exhausting. When you treat them as part of a long-term strategy, they become predictable, repeatable, and empowering.

This final chapter is about zooming out and locking everything together.

Why most creators plateau with brand deals

Most creators hit a ceiling because they never shift from reactive to intentional.

They:

- Wait for emails
- Say yes too fast
- Underprice themselves
- Overwork themselves
- Burn relationships quietly

None of that is because they lack talent. It is because they lack structure.

Structure is what turns luck into leverage.

The creator career flywheel

Everything in this book feeds into one loop:

Audience trust
→ Strong content
→ Aligned brand deals
→ Professional execution
→ Repeat opportunities
→ More leverage

Break any part of that loop and the system weakens.

Protect the loop and it compounds.

Why your reputation matters more than your metrics

Metrics fluctuate. Reputation sticks.

Brands remember:

- If you hit deadlines
- If you communicate clearly
- If you are easy to work with
- If you protect their brand
- If you protect your audience

A creator with slightly worse metrics but a strong reputation will out-earn a creator with bigger numbers and a bad reputation over time.

The boring habits that lead to success

There is nothing flashy about what works.

What works is:

- Tracking outreach
- Following up calmly

- Reading contracts
- Sending invoices correctly
- Delivering on time
- Being honest when things go wrong

These habits are not exciting. They are effective.

Mistakes you will make and why that's fine

You will:

- Undercharge early
- Say yes to bad fits
- Miss red flags
- Feel awkward negotiating
- Get ignored by brands you wanted badly

That is part of learning.

The goal is not to avoid mistakes entirely. The goal is to make them once, learn from them, and move forward smarter.

How to know you're doing it right

You are on the right track when:

- Deals feel easier, not harder

- Brands come back without pitching
- Negotiations feel calm
- Your audience trust stays intact
- Your income becomes more predictable

Progress often feels boring before it feels successful.

You do not need permission to charge fairly

This is worth repeating.

You do not need:

- Millions of followers
- Viral hits
- Validation from other creators

You need value, alignment, and professionalism.

If a brand is benefiting from your audience, your time has value.

Keep your identity bigger than your sponsors

Brands will come and go.

Your identity should not depend on:

- Who paid you last
- What product you promoted
- How much a deal was worth

Your content, voice, and audience are the foundation. Everything else sits on top of that.

Why patience wins in this space

Fast money exists. Long money lasts.

Creators who rush:

- Burn out
- Lose trust
- Plateau early

Creators who pace themselves:

- Build leverage
- Attract better brands
- Sleep better

You are building something. Treat it that way.

Final reminders to carry forward

Keep these close:

- Be professional even when others are not
- Ask questions before sending rates
- Read everything before signing
- Protect your audience first
- Follow up without desperation
- Say no without guilt
- Treat brands like clients, not saviors
- Play the long game

If you do those consistently, the rest takes care of itself.

Closing thoughts

You do not need to chase sponsorships.

You need to become the kind of creator brands want to work with repeatedly.

That is built through clarity, consistency, and care.

You already did the hardest part by creating something people care about. Everything in this book is about protecting and monetizing that without losing yourself along the way.

That is the real skill.

And now you have it.

About the Author

Matt Philie is a creator and strategist who has spent over a decade working with brands, agencies, and platforms on paid creator partnerships. He has managed and negotiated hundreds of sponsorships, and helped creators turn attention into predictable income. His work focuses on cutting through industry myths and teaching creators how brand deals actually work so they can stop undercharging, overdelivering, and guessing their way through negotiations.

You can connect with me on:
🌐 https://mattphilie.com